DUCKS

Title page: The boldly-patterned Common Shelduck, *Tadorna tadorna,* is found near the estuaries and salt lakes of Eurasia, where it differs from other ducks by nesting in holes, particularly rabbit burrows, in the ground. *Preceding pages:* Northern Pintails, *Anas acuta. These pages:* Ponds on the northern Great Plains and in the Prairie Provinces of Canada are the main nesting place for millions of ducks of many species. *Above:* Cinnamon Teal, *Anas cyanoptera.*

Common Goldeneye *Bucephala clangula.*

Mallard, *Anas platyrhynchos.*

North American Canvasback, *Aythya valisineria.*

DUCKS

SCOTT WEIDENSAUL

PORTLAND HOUSE

NEW YORK

This 1990 edition published by Portland House,
a division of dilithium Press, Ltd.
Distributed by Crown Publishers, Inc.
225 Park Avenue South, New York, New York 10003

ISBN 0517-03174-4
87654321

Printed and bound in Spain

For rights information about the photographs in
this book please contact:

The Image Bank
111 Fifth Avenue, New York, NY 10003

Author: Scott Weidensaul

Producer: Solomon M. Skolnick
Designer: Ann-Louise Lipman
Editor: Sara Colacurto
Production: Valerie Zars
Senior Picture Researcher: Edward Douglas
Editorial Assistant: Carol Raguso
Project Picture Researcher: Robert V. Hale

DÉP. LÉG. B-24.890-90

I N T R O D U C T I O N

One of the earliest representations of ducks in art comes from the wall of an Egyptian tomb. A man is shown aiming his throwing stick at flushing marsh birds, while his trained hunting cat makes a grab for a flying duck. Even in the fourteenth century B.C., the fortunes of people and waterfowl were linked.

That has become chillingly clear in recent years. Ducks need clean water, open space, and an unpolluted environment – the same general requirements that apply to humans. Sadly, many such resources have been squandered, and ducks and other wildlife are suffering at the loss.

But aside from their value as environmental indicators, ducks have always appealed to people for their grace, beauty, and freedom. The nearly 150 species of ducks found around the world range in behavior and appearance from comical to bizarre: A male Ruddy Duck, puffed up with courtship ardor, his bright blue bill held tightly against his russet chest, is unmistakably cute; a flight of Pintails racing the north wind, in an arc across the sky, steals one's breath away.

In the pages that follow, the intricacies of the natural history of ducks are explored, the words illustrated with striking photographs of duck species from around the globe. Just as there is no "typical" duck, there is no "typical" life story for these birds – some are stay-at-homes and others cross continents in migration. Some are solicitous parents, while some abandon their eggs to the care of others. Some are vegetarians, some are carnivores, and many are a mixture of both. But all are fascinating – as the ancient Egyptians would surely have agreed.

The Basic Duck

A duck is probably the most instantly recognizable bird in the world. Everyone knows what it takes to make one: short legs, webbed feet, a wide, flat bill, and that peculiar, waddling gait.

For some ducks, like the ubiquitous Mallard, that basic body plan marries neatly with reality – but not for all ducks, and it is in this diversity that so many duck aficionados find the greatest pleasure. Mergansers, for instance, have long, serrated bills. Whistling ducks have gracefully long legs that make them look more like geese than ducks. The stiff-tails, including the pert Ruddy Duck of North America, resemble wind-up toys more than they do real birds.

Defining what is *not* a duck can be even stickier. Why are geese and swans not considered ducks, even though all three share the family *Anatidae*? It certainly isn't a matter of size; several arctic subspecies of the Canada goose are scarcely larger than Mallards, and the white Ross' goose may actually be smaller. Proportion plays a role – geese and swans tend to have longer legs and necks – but the whistling ducks of the subtropics blur that distinction hopelessly.

The truth is, there are no hard-and-fast rules on what makes a duck a duck, just a collection of generalities and a flock of exceptions. Most ducks are small (under two feet in length and four pounds in weight), with short necks, webbed feet, spatulate bills, and an affinity for water. Unlike geese and swans, in most (but not all) duck species, the male is more brightly colored than his mate.

Ducks are usually divided into two broad categories: the "puddle" ducks, or dabbling ducks, which include such familiar species as the Mallard, Pintail, and Black Duck; and the diving ducks like the Canvasback, Scaup, and Redhead. Most birders and waterfowl experts further separate some of the divers into a third group, the sea ducks – big, heavy birds like the Scoter, Eider, and Harlequin Duck, which are found on saltwater at least part of the year. Mergansers and whistling ducks are so unlike any other types of waterfowl that they usually each are placed in their own subgroups, as are the stiff-tails, which in North America includes only the Ruddy and Masked Ducks.

Puddle ducks are slim, with legs set near the mid-point of the body so they can easily move on dry land. These are the ducks of freshwater, for the most part, at home in quiet backwaters, wooded ponds, and prairie marshes. Feeding is done in shallow water, usually involving nothing more than a "tip up," with tail skyward and feet thrashing while they grub for insects, seeds, or roots in the muddy bottom. They are capable of diving, especially if pursued by a predator, but they prefer to take their chances in flight. They are agile and spring straight up into the air when startled – an explosive eruption into flight accompanied by frightened squawks and a spray of water, the perfect get-away for the closed-in spaces many of them frequent.

Divers, on the other hand, are more cumbersome on land: their legs are set far back on the body, making walking awkward and difficult. Yet while this is a disadvantage on dry ground, it is a plus in the water, for diving ducks can exert tremendous strength with their legs. As their name implies, diving ducks frequently swim to great depths for food;

Oldsquaws have been caught in fishing nets almost 90 feet deep, and diving ducks in Europe have been snagged at more than 200 feet below the water's surface.

Divers generally stick to big water – large lakes, big rivers, the sea – where the horizon is flat, the wind slices with an icy edge in winter, and there is plenty of open water for a running start. Divers cannot jump nimbly into the air like puddle ducks; they must build steam, flapping madly as they run across the surface, leaving a trail of splashy footprints in their wake. Once aloft, however, they are among the swiftest of ducks. The Canvasback and Oldsquaw have both been timed at more than 70 miles per hour in level flight, and a speed of 80 miles per hour is claimed for one Red-breasted Merganser. While these speeds don't compare to the 200 miles per hour achieved by the peregrine falcon, they clearly demonstrate that these are very fast animals.

There are other small but significant differences between divers and puddle ducks. The bills of the divers are generally shorter and stouter than those of puddle ducks and are better suited for ripping mussels loose from their rocky moorings. Also, while all ducks have three webbed toes, the fourth rear toe of a diver is lobed, presumably for greater power when swimming.

A further word about a duck's feet. Many a waterfowl hunter has, after shivering in insulated waders on a frigid winter day in the marsh, wondered how a duck can tolerate bare legs in such brutal conditions, much less sit contently through the night on an ice floe. The reason is the construction of their feet and legs. Unlike human appendages, in which the skeletal framework is covered in a thick sheath of muscle, a bird's legs are quite literally skin and bone (and tendons). Blood circulation is minimal since there is no muscle to supply with oxygen, so a duck's legs and feet are exceptionally tolerant of the cold.

The hallmark of any bird is its feathers, and ducks are certainly no exception. Waterfowl have extremely thick, dense plumage, which provides both superior insulation and excellent waterproofing. But all feathers are not created equal – there are different varieties, each suited for a different purpose on the duck's body. Most of the visible body plumage is made up of contour feathers, or vaned feathers. A central, hollow quill grows out of a muscular pocket in the skin; from either side of the flattened quill come sheets of webbing that form the vane of the feather. A close look reveals that the vane is in turn made of individual filaments, called barbules. The barbs can be separated, then "zipped" back together again – often a part of a bird's preening process. Under extreme magnification, it can be seen that the barbs are themselves covered with microscopic hooks that connect each barb to its neighbor. The result is a light and flexible but extremely strong structure perfectly suited for flight.

The flight feathers of the wings and tails are the largest, best-developed contour feathers on the duck. The stiffest are the primary feathers, which grow from the wingtip to the fold at the bird's "elbow." From the fold to the body are the secondaries, which are a bit more flexible, since they do not have to tolerate the extremes of pressure in flight that the primaries must endure; linking the secondaries to the body are the tertials, another set of limber contour feathers.

The coloration of ducks is unique among birds because the secondaries of most duck species, particularly the puddle ducks, are brilliantly iridescent. This distinctive patch of color is known as the speculum – bright blue on a Mallard, purple on a Black Duck, shimmering bronze on a drake Pintail. Unlike the brown or black coloration of the body feathers, the speculum's color comes not from pigment, but from the structure of the feather itself. Specialized cells in the barbules break and refract sunlight, intensifying some wavelengths and nullifying others to produce some of the most vibrant colors in the animal kingdom.

Not all ducks possess a speculum, diving ducks, for example, do not, but the wing pattern of each species is unique. Each year, the United States Fish and Wildlife Service asks selected duck hunters to mail in the wings of the ducks they shoot; the wings are identified and counted as a way of tabulating the annual sport kill.

The contour feathers of the duck's body make it streamlined, allowing air to flow over the duck smoothly, with a minimum of friction. They also provide a waterproof covering for the down feathers – from a commercial viewpoint, the most important variety of feather on a duck. Where the barbules of a contour feather lock together to form sheets, down feather barbs are free agents, lacking hooks and unity. Each down feather forms its own little sphere, trapping air within its gauzy barbs. This captured air is what allows the down to make the duck at once buoyant and warm, for air is the best insulator of all. The down of the northern species is especially thick and fine, and a major industry has grown up in Iceland, involving the collection of eiderdown from the nests of Common and King Eiders. The females pluck huge quantities of the brownish down from their breasts, forming from these feathers what must rank as the world's most luxuriant nests; down harvesters collect a portion from each nest, making certain to leave enough to insulate the hatchlings. The birds are not harmed by the collection; in fact, the islanders have a strong economic incentive to protect the ducks.

In terms of numbers, a duck's contour feathers, although they are bigger, make up a smaller percentage of the total than do down and other, smaller feather types. A duck of average size – a Mallard, for instance – probably carries about 12,000 feathers on its body, from the largest primaries to the smallest, bristlelike filoplumes. Scattered through the contour feathers, filoplumes serve no insulating or flight function, but because they are linked to sensitive nerves, it is believed that they provide information on the position of the larger feathers, as well as on air currents and pressure. Instinctively translating what the filoplumes report, the duck can make tiny corrections in the position of its contour feathers, achieving maximum efficiency in the air.

All ducks have a large, well-developed uropygial, or preen, gland on the rump just above the tail; when the area is plucked, the gland shows as a bump, crowned with a tuft of short, dense feathers. Oil is secreted by the gland, a mixture of fat, wax, and natural acids that serves the duck admirably as a waterproofing agent. Preening is an important part of the duck's day, and the birds invest a great deal of time and energy in doing it right. The duck works systematically, squeezing a small amount of oil from the preen gland, then working it carefully into its feathers, which are drawn through the bill with a gentle nibbling action.

Preening accomplishes several tasks at once – it removes dirt and debris from the feathers, realigns the feather barbules, and spreads a new sheen of oil throughout the plumage. A well-preened duck fairly glows in the sun, from the combination of healthy plumage and glistening oil. The preen oil may even help the bird synthesize Vitamin D (those whose uropygial glands are removed may develop rickets), and it is critical in maintaining the bill and leg scales, which are made of keratin, the same as the feathers.

The one area that the duck cannot preen efficiently with its bill is, of course, its own head. In this case, toenails seem to serve as an acceptable substitute for the duck's preening bill; the duck will vigorously scratch every section of its head, with particular attention paid to the throat and the auriculars, the feathers behind the eye covering the duck's ear holes. Preening ducks go at the task with gusto, constantly fluffing, shaking, and flapping; it is obvious that preening is a pleasant undertaking and usually a sign of a bird completely at ease. Loose feathers drift on the wind or skate along the water, pushed by the slightest breeze, and during the molting season they may pile up in windrows along the leeward shore.

Despite the effort ducks reserve for preening, it is instantly obvious to an observer that their greatest enthusiasm is for eating. Little wonder, for a bird's metabolism is quite high, requiring plenty of food. Although a duck doesn't have the insatiable furnace of a hummingbird or a chickadee, it requires many calories to grow feathers, lay on fat, and maintain an even body temperature.

Diets vary widely among ducks. Even among the closely related puddle ducks of the genus *Anas*, variety is the rule. Mallards take mostly seeds, along with aquatic plants, insects, tiny crustaceans, acorns, and domestic grain. The rare Mottled Duck of the Gulf Coast, which may be nothing more than a Mallard subspecies, relies to a much greater extent on animal matter, especially tiny shrimp, isopods, and mollusks. Gadwalls feed in deeper water than other puddle ducks, often diving to beds of aquatic plants; Wigeons are known for eating lots of greenery, including grass, but they often pirate food from other ducks, including Gadwalls, that bring up fronds of plants from the bottom.

Perhaps the oddest feeding adaptation among the puddle duck is seen in the bill of the Northern Shoveler, a small teal with a vastly outsized beak that is longer than its head and considerably broader than most duck bills. While the Shoveler will often feed like other ducks, it can also strain out tiny organisms by filtering muddy water through layers of *lamellae*, comblike structures along the inner edge of both bills. Other puddle ducks have lamellae, but only in the Shoveler have they reached such a pinnacle of development; the Shoveler also has an unusually long intestinal tract, allowing it to more easily digest minute animals.

Among divers, animal matter plays a greater role in the diet, although some, like Canvasbacks and Redheads, feed most heavily on underwater plants. (For this reason, Cans and Redheads are often prized as table birds by hunters, whereas most other divers are scorned for their fishy taste.) Greater Scaups wintering along the coast feed predominantly on clams, mussels, and other mollusks, while Lesser Scaups take a greater proportion of plants. Although preference varies among divers, most of the sea ducks feed almost exclusively on shellfish and crustaceans and, as a result of this, their flesh has a heavy, rank odor.

Goldeneyes and Buffleheads, more so than most ducks, have a dietary split from summer to winter. On their breeding grounds on northern lakes, they eat large quantities of insects, freshwater shrimp, and crayfish (with the Buffleheads adding lots of plant matter to the mix), but when they migrate to their wintering grounds along the coast, they switch over, to a large degree, to shellfish.

Mergansers are the only ducks that routinely feed on fish and, not surprisingly, their bills reflect their tastes. Rather than the broad flattened bill one expects on a duck, the three species of North American mergansers have long, thin beaks, lined with toothlike serrations that do an admirable job of holding slippery fish. Insects and crustaceans round out their diet, especially among young mergansers. In fact, aquatic insects are such a good source of protein that most young ducks eat them, regardless of what their adult diet may be. In lakes suffering the ill effects of acid precipitation, the insects are among the first to disappear, dooming many clutches of ducklings.

Ducks perceive the world in much the same way as humans, but there are some differences. Ducks have excellent vision, and they use this sense more than any other. In proportion to its head, a duck's eyes are quite large (especially when compared to a mammal's), but still smaller than those of a hawk or owl. The eyes permit color vision, although experiments have shown that these birds cannot distinguish subtle colors nearly as well as people can – which may account for the brilliance of their plumage. A duck's eyes are more sensitive to movement, however, especially along a horizontal band of the retina; in open-land birds, like ducks, this zone of sensitivity is parallel to the horizon when the duck holds its head in a normal, resting position, thus affording the bird the greatest chance of spotting danger.

As anyone who has opened their eyes underwater knows, an eye that functions properly in air gives distorted vision in water. Diving ducks, which need clear vision above and beneath the waves, compensate with a form of natural contact lens. All birds have a *nictitans* with each eye, a translucent "third eyelid" that can be flicked back to clean and protect the organ, but in diving ducks the nictitans has a clear, lens-shaped window that corrects the distortion caused by water.

The sense of smell is poor in most birds, although experiments have shown that some species, like pigeons, may navigate in part by smell. As might be expected, the sense of taste in birds is also poorly developed, and most puddle ducks find their food more by touch than taste or smell as they grub through the sediment of a pond bottom or sandbar, relying on receptor nerves at the tip of the bill to tell them when they have found food. The duck's hearing, while developed, is not used to detect predators, since most of their natural predators, like the peregrine falcon, make a soundless attack.

Worldwide, there are between 140 and 148 species of waterfowl. (The number varies depending on whether some closely related forms are considered full species or merely subspecies, and even the experts disagree on that issue.) Originally, North America had 35 species of breeding ducks, but the extinction of the Labrador Duck in the 1870's reduced the tally by one. Additionally, vagrants from Europe, Asia, Central America, and the Caribbean regularly show up far from home, adding another nine or 10 species to the list of possibilities.

The Labrador Duck remains a mystery. Even when still extant, it was an enigma to early ornithologists; like others, John James Audubon searched for its nests in Labrador without success, and his famous painting was based on specimens someone else had shot. The duck was found along the Northeast coast in winter, sometimes as far south as Virginia, but mostly in the waters off Long Island. A handsome bird, the male Pied Duck (as it was also known) was black, with white wings and chest, a black collar, white face, and black cap. The bill was orange and black, and more spatulate than that of most diving ducks. This fact, plus old accounts of it feeding on shallow shoals, has led to speculation that it sifted small shellfish from the sand, rather than from the water like most sea ducks.

The flesh of the Labrador Duck tasted strongly of fish and was never sought out by market gunners. The only reasonable explanation for its disappearance is that eggers and feather-hunters, who pillaged the seabird colonies of northeast Canada in the nineteenth century, wiped out this beautiful bird, which apparently was uncommon to begin with.

Interestingly, there is very little difference between the ducks of North America and the ducks of Eurasia. With the Bering land bridge a recent memory, geologically speaking, and with ducks capable of long-distance flight, it is no surprise that many species are found across much of the Northern Hemisphere. The Mallard; Gadwall; Pintail; Green-winged Teal; Shoveler; Common, King, and Steller's Eiders; Red-breasted and Common Mergansers; Common Goldeneye; and Greater Scaup are all found in Europe as well as North America. The Harlequin Duck and Barrow's Goldeneye live in Iceland, not yet having made the leap to the Continent.

The American and Eurasian Wigeon are separate species but very closely related, as are the Eurasian Pochard and North American Redhead, and the Ring-necked Duck and Tufted Duck. Confusing matters more is the question of names: an Oldsquaw in North America is a Long-tailed Duck in Britain; a Common Merganser here is a Goosander there; and what a Long Island birder calls a White-wing Scoter, a European calls a Velvet Scoter. The name-swapping highlights the importance of the binomial system of nomenclature, usually referred to as "scientific names." The two-part, latinized name given each living thing is unique, and unlike common, or vernacular names, does not change from continent to continent. Thus, an Oldsquaw is always *Clangula hyemalis* to a biologist, whatever the locals may call the bird.

Despite the close kinship between the ducks of Eurasia and North America, there are some differences. Ducks evolved sometime in the Eocene period, roughly 50 million years ago (or at least that is when their fragile bones first appear in the fossil record). Since then, the continental drift has opened and closed barriers to travel by even the swiftest fliers, cutting off some populations and creating the isolation in which evolution occurs. So even though the Green-winged Teal of Europe and the U.S. are considered one species, *Anas crecca,* there are distinct, if minor, differences between the two. The European subspecies, *A.c. crecca,* has a white edge to the scapular feathers of the back that the North American sub-species, *A.C. carolinensis,* lacks, while a drake *carolinensis* has a vertical white bar on its side that its European cousin does not. It is thus, by small degrees, that evolutionary change occurs; given the continued separation of the two subspecies – and a lot more time – the two forms of the Green-winged Teal will probably develop far greater differences of color and form, until they may one day be what we will consider distinct species.

The Seasons of Birth

It is late winter on the salt marsh, and a bitter northwest wind flings itself across the flat expanse of dead cordgrass. Meander-ing through the brown marsh, sluggish tidal creeks rimmed with ice empty into a small cove, where the wind has raked the gray water into whitecaps.

Bobbing among the waves, a flock of Buffleheads ignore the weather, which holds a hint of snow and nothing at all of spring. Yet each day has been fractionally longer than the one before it, and the changing daylight has caused a surge of hormones through their systems. The thermometer says it is still winter, but to the ducks, the time for courtship has arrived.

The little males, round as butterballs and not much bigger, flare their head feathers, an act that in other ducks would simply raise a crest, but which in the Bufflehead makes the entire head swell like a black-and-white ball.

Males square off against each other, some pumping their heads up and down in a ritualistic movement, while others take off for short display flights, their white wing patches flash-ing like semaphore flags over the pewter ocean water. Fights break out here and there between competing drakes, scrap-ping and tussling in a flurry of wingbeats and pecking bills.

The summer nesting season is still months away, but already the Buffleheads are feeling the urge to pair up – an urge that strikes ducks earlier than almost any other group of birds except hawks and owls. Unlike geese and swans, which frequently mate for life (or at least for long stretches of time), the bonds that ducks form are far more temporary; in some cases, there is no bond at all beyond the momentary union of mating. In others, the attraction may last from one year to the next.

Such is the case with the Buffleheads, which develop unusually strong pair bonds for ducks. They also show an exceptional fidelity to their nest sites, returning year after year to the same small lake, even to the same tree, for Buffleheads are cavity nesters, seeking out old woodpecker holes or natural hollows in trees to make their nests. As soon as the ice melts on the boreal lakes of Canada, the Rockies, and Alaska, the Buffleheads arrive, staking out territories that they vigor-ously defend against other Buffleheads, and even against other duck species. In such battles they usually are able to evict intruders, but often lose to determined pairs of Goldeneyes,

a larger species that also covets the scarce nest holes.

Tree cavities, whether the result of disease or a wood-pecker's excavations, are never common, making the selection of a new site more problematic for a Bufflehead than for ground-nesting species that need only to gather a pile of vegetation together for a nest. Still, female Buffleheads can be very selective in choosing a nest hole and show a decided preference for flicker cavities, which are usually just barely big enough for the pudgy ducks to squeeze into; it may be that by choosing the tightest fit possible, they make it harder for predators that might otherwise raid their nests. For the same reason, trees that are standing in water, such as those killed by a new beaver dam, are also preferred.

The only refurbishing the new home receives is a layer of down, plucked from the female's breast and compressed to form a thick, insulating cover over the damp wood pulp of the hole. With the nest finished, each morning for about two weeks the female will slip into the hole at dawn and lay a single glossy, bone-white egg, then slip away again. Not until the clutch is complete – usually around a dozen eggs – will she settle in to begin incubating. This way, the embryos wait in a state of arrested development until incubation begins, so that all hatch at virtually the same time.

Incubation is solely the responsibility of the female, whose mate takes over all territorial defense, serving as a watchdog and raising the roof if a predator like a marten comes too close to the nest. Taking brief breaks only to feed, the female will incubate for about one month, keeping the eggs at a constant temperature as the embryos develop. In the last day before hatching, the chicks may become active, moving within the shell; the female may respond with soft calls, encouraging the chicks to begin the laborious process of hatching. Armed with a tiny egg tooth (really just a sharp, horny protrusion on the tip of the beak), the chicks peck their way through the hard shell, first opening a little hole called the pip. From pipping to the final release from the shell may take a chick four or five hours, leaving it utterly exhausted.

The Bufflehead chicks that emerge from their eggs are quite unlike the naked, helpless babies of a robin or swallow. Clothed in a thick coat of down, eyes open, and able to feed themselves from birth, the young of all ducks come into the world in an advanced state of development. They are what biologists refer to as *precocial* young, and while they still require constant guarding and frequent brooding, they are substantially more independent that the *altricial* chicks of songbirds and raptors.

Many ground-nesting ducks abandon their nests almost as soon as the chicks hatch, since they are most vulnerable on land. Relatively safe within their tree nest, the Buffleheads will stay inside for a day or two as the young recover from the ordeal of hatching and learn how to coordinate their movements. Then they simply scramble out of the tree cavity and into the wide world, following their mother, who can fly – even though they cannot. While she glides to a graceful landing on the ground below, the chicks must jump into thin air, smacking down with an impact that looks more damaging than it actually is. Most Bufflehead nests are rather low, less than 10 feet high, but the chicks of the Wood Duck routinely plummet 50 or 60 feet to the ground, parachuting with their stubby wings and big feet, and bouncing like rubber balls when they hit, none the worse for the wear.

Because Bufflehead chicks are so active from birth, the female has only to lead her brood to places where food is abundant. On quiet June mornings on the beaver ponds and backwater coves of Canada's spruce forest, it is common to see a female Bufflehead, gray against the white mist, cutting ripples in the calm water, followed by a dozen or more fluffy ducklings. Although their adult plumage is still many weeks away, the chicks are already waterproof; in fact, their biggest problem is that they are too buoyant and cannot dive for more than a second or two before popping like corks back to the surface. Still, they are able to forage for backswimmers, damselfly larvae, and the myriad of other aquatic insects and crustaceans that swarm in the water shallows. Their mother has only to show them food the first time, and instinct kicks in.

There is, of course, danger as well as food in the northern woods, and almost every duck family is slowly whittled down as the weeks pass. Northern pike engulf the newborns (and occasionally even the adults); smallmouth bass and other large fish, and even snapping turtles, may also take a stray duckling. Death may come from the sky – herring gulls, goshawks, merlins, or great horned owls often prey on the young – or from land, in the form of mink, weasels, fishers, foxes, bobcats, or other mammalian predators. It is a hard world in which to grow up, and many don't make it, becoming, instead, fuel for the vast northern food web. Those that survive the first five weeks of flightlessness eventually gain their first juvenile plumage, which for both sexes resembles the adult female's. More importantly, they get their flight feathers, which greatly improves their odds of survival.

If the Bufflehead represents those ducks with a rather limited range and specific nesting requirements, the Mallard is the shining example of a reproductive generalist, able to nest in virtually every habitat, from prairie marshlands to urban parks, from streamside willow thickets in the arid West to arctic tundra ponds. They are as at home building their nests among the tulips of a suburban flowerbed as they are in a wilderness setting, so it is no surprise that the Mallard is the most successful duck in North America; indeed, in the world, since it is also found in Europe, Asia, Central America, and parts of Africa and has been introduced to Australia and New Zealand.

Unlike the Bufflehead, the Mallard makes no lasting pair bond that survives the years: at best, Mallards are seasonally monogamous, but in most cases the male will abandon the female after she begins nesting to look for another unattached hen. As the nesting season progresses and the number of unmated females dwindles, the bachelor flocks may become increasingly aggressive. One of the most unpleasant scenes for a birder to witness is that of three or four drakes simultaneously attempting to mate with one female; if this takes place in the water, the unfortunate hen may be forced under the surface by the combined weight of the attackers, and may even drown.

Mallards have a set of ritualized courtship displays, many of which have their origins in aggressive behavior but have been modified over thousands of years into something alluring rather than hostile. Bird behaviorists have studied the displays of Mallards extensively, since the species is common and

rather tame, and consequently, we know more about the Mallard's "body language" than that of any other duck, and possibly any other wild bird. The displays are rather subtle – nothing as dramatic as the side-by-side, skittering "dance" of the Fulvous Whistling Duck, or the kicking display of the Common Goldeneye. Instead, the male may swim with his neck stretched out, low to the water, or dip his bill to the surface and snap it up, showering his prospective mate with water; such displays are often choreographed among several ducks, each performing in almost perfect unison.

Ornithologists have coined descriptive names for each display: the "water-flick," the "head-up-tail-up," the "tail-shake," the "grunt-whistle." Males do most of the courting, but among Mallards, as with many species of ducks, the females have a separate set of displays that they can use to entice an unwilling male or signal her availability. One female specialty is known as an "incite display," in which she quickly tosses her head back and to the side, over and over again, especially when being followed by intruding drakes; her mate responds by driving off the interlopers. A "nodding" display by unattached females spurs displaying drakes to even greater exhibitions.

The courtship displays of birds are an important isolating factor, preventing hybridization among closely related species, since members of one species usually won't respond to another species' displays. Among ducks, especially puddle ducks, however, the system occasionally breaks down because many species have very similar displays. The 10 North American puddle ducks all belong to the genus *Anas* and are capable of producing hybrid young. Some hybrids are even rather common: Black Duck/Mallard crosses, for instance, or Mallard/Pintails and Blue-winged/Cinnamon Teal mixes, to say nothing of the genetic mishmash that results wherever wild Mallards and domestic ducks are found, such as in municipal parks. Novice birders are forever finding "rare" ducks that are nothing more than oddball hybrids – but even experts can be suckered. In 1822, Audubon painted what he thought was a new species, the Bemaculated Duck, which he later named for his friend Thomas Brewer. He suspected even then that his new discovery wasn't quite legitimate, and he was right; "Brewer's Duck" was only a hybrid of a Mallard and Gadwall, with the latter's grayish body and a touch of the former's green head.

A Mallard drake will pugnaciously attack another male that approaches his mate, but neither member of the pair defends a breeding territory, and in good habitat, Mallards can be found nesting within a few feet of each other. The hen has none of the Bufflehead's choosiness in selecting a nest site. The majority of nests, to be sure, are found near water – in rushes or sedges along the margins of a pond, in marshes, beside the banks of small streams, or in some other reasonably normal location. But more than any other duck, Mallards have a tendency to choose erratic spots to nest, including building rooftops, vegetable gardens, window wells, beneath outdoor stairways, inside beached canoes, and, in Europe, often inside hollow trees. In fact, nearby water is not even an absolute requirement for the Mallard.

Even those drakes that do not desert their mates when incubation begins play no role in caring for the eggs or chicks, and when the young hatch, it is invariably the hen with which they are seen. (Many people, spotting a drake, hen, and flotilla of chicks on a park pond, mistake the group for a family, not realizing that the male is almost certainly an uninvited third party hoping to mate with the hen.) The clutch of eggs usually numbers between six and 12 – a large number when compared to most birds, but par for the course among ducks. Waterfowl and other gamebirds have long been known for their high reproductive potential, no doubt evolved in ducks because of a variety of pressures: the need to compensate, in the case of a single brood, for losses to predators and a long migration, and to rebuild the population quickly after drought.

A mated hen whose nest has been destroyed, or that for some reason hasn't built one, will occasionally "dump" her eggs in the nest of another hen. Unusual behavior for Mallards, it is far more common in other species – particularly the Redhead.

Redheads are diving ducks, summer residents of the famous prairie pothole region of the northern Plains, where the retreating glaciers of the last ice age left the landscaped pockmarked with thousands of marshes, lakes, and jewel-like ponds. The potholes are exceptionally rich in plant and animal life and annually support more than half of North America's duck population, making it the richest duck-producing area in the world.

With the coming of spring, the Redheads return from the southern U.S. and Mexico to their breeding grounds in the prairies. The Bufflehead's preference for spruce-lined lakes and the Mallard's tolerance for suburbia is not for them – they like wide open spaces, big marshes and sloughs where the only things seen on the horizon are the fuzzy purple flowers of the blazing star, rising high on spikes above the prairie. Redhead hens show a preference for stands of emergent vegetation like bulrushes or cattails, building their nests deep in a clump of reeds. Woven from pieces of dead marsh grass, the nest is a big basket lined with down. But if the form of the nest is standard among Redheads, the female's nesting behavior is decidedly not.

Many follow the "normal" route, laying 10 or 15 eggs and brooding them faithfully though incubation. Others lay part of their clutch in their own nest, but seek out the nests of other ducks – including other species – and lay a few eggs among the host's. Still other hen Redheads skip nesting altogether and deposit all of their eggs in the nest of other ducks. Canvas-backs and other Redheads are among the most frequently parasitized species, although scaups, teal, and the Mallard are also victims; in one Utah marsh, nearly 80 percent of the Cinnamon Teal nests contained at least one Redhead egg.

No one is really sure how the Redhead's parasitic behavior started, and whether the mix of parasitic and nonparasitic females means that this is a relatively recent development that has yet to spread to the entire species. There is a strong natural selection against parasitism, however: research has shown that the eggs of nonparasitic Redheads are more likely to hatch and result in fledgling young than those dumped in another nest, even another Redhead nest.

Worldwide, there are ducks with still odder breeding habits. The Shelducks of Europe (somewhat intermediate between geese and true ducks) habitually use rabbit burrows for their nests, although they will not spurn old fox dens or a shallow, natural scrape. Once the chicks hatch, they follow the hen to the water, but instead of staying in a discreet family unit, most broods tend to bunch up into créches, in which a few adults may ride herd over dozens and dozens of ducklings.

The infant stage is prolonged in waterfowl; despite their advanced development at hatching, it takes them much longer to reach the degree of self-sufficiency that, in song-birds, is attained only three or four weeks after birth. In most songbirds, fledging (the point at which flight becomes possible) naturally comes at about the same time as the chick's departure from the nest. For ducks, which leave the nest almost immediately, fledging is a less clear-cut point, which may come as soon as five weeks from birth for the slow-growing Common Merganser. As the chicks lose their baby down and acquire adult plumage, both sexes closely resemble the hens. Young males will not gain their full breeding plumage until fall or, in some cases, late winter.

In midsummer, the drakes also undergo a remarkable transformation. Within just a few weeks, they molt out most of their feathers, replacing their colorful breeding plumage with "eclipse" plumage, which in most cases is almost indistinguishable from the drab hen's. Also lost in a fell swoop are the primary feathers of the wings, rendering the ducks flightless, which might explain why the drakes would want to share the hen's camouflaging pattern.

For birders, differentiating between hens and eclipse drakes can be maddening; the differences are there, but they are subtle and slight. The Mallard drake in eclipse, for instance, has a breast that is a marginally richer chestnut tone, and his bill is drab olive, instead of the hen's orange-and-black one. The eclipse may last as little as a month or two, followed by a second body molt into the breeding plumage again, although some species, like the Northern Shoveler, delay the appearance of full "nuptial" plumage until the beginning of spring. For the Shelduck, the onset of the molt signals a unique migration, in which virtually the entire British population flies across the Channel to the estuaries of the Heligoland Bight on the coast of northern Germany. There they molt their flight feathers in the comparative safety of these low-lying, marshy islands, returning to their breeding grounds again after the new primaries and secondaries have grown in.

Invisible Highways

It is a sight that cannot fail to stir the heart – flocks of waterfowl heading south, hung beneath a cloud-flecked October sky, rowing through the air on flashing wings. But if the sight of migrating ducks brings a thrill to the grounded humans below, it also touches another, more unsettling chord, for the southward flight of ducks and geese has been a signal of impending winter since the end of the last ice age. Even insulated by modern life, we shiver a bit with the fore-knowledge that migration brings.

That aside, the passage of waterfowl is a majestic spectacle, stitching together the continents into seamless unity. Political boundaries fall into insignificance. To the birds, only survival matters.

Across most of the Northern Hemisphere, the breeding season reaches its peak in June and, except in the Arctic, nesting activity drops dramatically through July. Most ducks raise only one brood – the amount of time involved in incubation, and the long period before fledging, preclude any more. So late summer is a time of indolence, molting, laying on fat reserves, and honing survival skills among the young – a time to prepare.

Yet by the end of summer, the ducks are anything but at ease. Biologists call it *zugunruhe*, a German word meaning migratory restlessness. Watching a flock of ducks in late August, one can see it at work; the birds are edgy, springing into the air without provocation, making short circling flights around the marsh. They feed frenetically, never seeming to relax. Tension thrums across the air from bird to bird.

Just as with the onset of courtship in the spring, and the molt in midsummer, the restlessness is the work of hormones – prolactin from the pituitary, and corticosterone from other endocrine glands. Hormones also stimulate the duck's body to begin laying on fat reserves, although the percentage of fat a duck accumulates does not even match that in the body of a fall songbird, which may weigh half again as much as its breeding weight.

Even the hormones need a trigger, though, and that trigger is sunlight. The ratio of sun to darkness changes each day in the temperate zone, from the short days of winter to the lingering twilight of summer. Biologists have found that this ratio, known as the photoperiod, controls virtually all aspects of a bird's life – from when it comes into breeding condition to when it gets the itch to migrate – by triggering the release of various hormones.

Even though the duck must be in the proper physiological condition to migrate, it is the weather that provides the final push. In the fall, a cell of high pressure drifting down from the Arctic, bringing with it clear blue skies, cool temperatures, and a brisk northwest wind, is often the spark. However, the movement south is not universal: there is a clear distinction between the migratory timing of immatures and adults. The old image of an experienced elder leading the flocks south is wrong; in virtually all species, the young birds, hatched just a few short months earlier, actually make the trip south *before* their parents, following an instinctive, genetically imprinted map. Even in the handful of species, like the Pintail and Blue-winged Teal, in which the adult males migrate first, different age classes (and even different sexes) migrate on their own.

Among many birds, not just ducks, the adults linger the longest on the breeding grounds, finally being chased out by the steadily worsening weather that winter's approach brings. Along the Atlantic seaboard, the gales of early winter carry on their breakneck winds the big, mature, male Black Ducks with their bright crimson legs. These birds are so much more robust than the females and immatures that turn-of-the-century waterfowlers called them Red-legged Ducks, thinking they were another species entirely.

For creatures as wonderfully insulated as ducks, it is not the cold itself that forces them out – it is the growing scarcity of food and open water. A duck sleeping through the night in the middle of a pond or lake is as safe as a wild animal can be, subject to attack only from great horned owls, otters, and perhaps an adventuresome mink. When the lake freezes, however – assuming that a sudden cold snap doesn't lock the birds in fresh ice, as sometimes happens – the duck must leave because its sanctuary has been sealed off.

For the flying bird, unbound by the constraints of trails and terrain, the quickest route between two points would seem to be a straight line. And to a degree it is, but even for a high-flying duck, the lay of the land far below exerts a powerful influence on the route taken. So-called leading lines on the landscape – rivers, valleys, lakeshores, the coast, mountain ranges – all conspire to nudge the migrants one way or another as they seek the path of least resistance. As a result, the chaotic surge of southward-bound ducks quickly takes on a more ordered flow, tributaries joining to form rivers in the sky.

These invisible highways, called "flyways," are hereditary routes that join the breeding grounds of the north with the warmer, gentler regions of the south. In North America, where their existence was first recognized and the name coined, there are four major flyways: the Atlantic, Mississippi, Central, and Pacific. Over the years there have been many maps drawn of the four, neatly funneling waterfowl across the continent – too neatly, in fact, for the flyways are much less coherent than any map would indicate. The Mississippi Flyway, for example, draws on ducks from the span of the Arctic, from Alaska's North Slope to the Ungava of Quebec. Ducks that use the Atlantic Flyway may come from as far west as the Northwest Territories, crossing paths with birds bred just one tundra pond over, but that will follow the Pacific Flyway south instead. Even at their midpoints there is considerable overlap between flyways, and it is an almost random judgment as to where one ends and another begins.

Although it has long been clear where the major wintering grounds lay, and to a degree what the routes taken were, the full extent of the flyway system did not come to light until the first half of the twentieth century, when banding became common. An old technique (Audubon tied silver wire to the legs of songbirds in Pennsylvania to prove that they returned to the same territory each year), banding was not organized on a formal, international scale until the 1920's. Trained banders capture wild birds and crimp light, aluminum alloy bands around their legs, each imprinted with a unique series of numbers and the address of the Bird Banding Laboratory in Washington, D.C. Once banded, a bird goes from being utterly anonymous to a recognizable individual, and if it is found dead or recaptured, its lifespan, migratory route, and much more can be inferred.

Ducks are undoubtedly the most frequently banded of wild birds, since their recreational value is high enough to warrant a great deal of attention from biologists, and they are easy to capture in large numbers, especially during their flightless summer molt. They also have perhaps the highest recovery rate of any group of banded birds, since so many are taken by hunters each fall. As a result, a clear picture of migration paths and breeding and wintering grounds has come to light, and research continues to refine these images.

Thanks in large part to banding, scientists now know that female ducks have a greater loyalty to their birthplace than do males, so that among species that pair up on the wintering grounds, the males tend to follow the females home, rather than the other way around. Because of band returns, it is known that most ducks take about a month to complete their southward migration, but considerably less time to retrace the route in the spring, when the mating urge presumably eggs them on. It is known that many hens return to the same tree hole or grassy hummock year after year to build their nests, that Blue-winged Teal from Manitoba winter in Venezuela, and that a Mallard can live at least 23 years (as one banded in Oregon in 1948 proved).

Banding and other tracking technologies have brought to light some of the subtleties of the flyway system, as well as some of the exceptions. A major study of Canvasbacks showed that the species follows its own peculiar route each fall, rather than going with the flow. Most Canvasbacks nest in the northern prairies, and a large percentage of the population winters in the Chesapeake and other Atlantic bays. To get there, the Cans travel east, funneling through the Great Lakes (where some stay for the winter), and on to the ocean. Others peel off the main route, however, and head south along the Mississippi River, where they in turn settle in for the season. Still others pick up the Central and Pacific flyways, although not in numbers nearly as large as those that migrate east.

Banding may highlight the complexity of the migratory flyways, but it does nothing to explain *how* those pathways evolved. Such a discussion is not limited to ducks; biologists have puzzled over the equally impressive travels of songbirds, seabirds, raptors, and almost every other group of Temperate Zone birds. There are two schools of thought, referred to as the Southern Home and Northern Home theories.

According to the Southern Home theory, most of the Northern Hemisphere's birds were originally southern, living far from the Pleistocene glaciers, which rendered much of North America and Eurasia an icy waste for millennia at a time. When the ice sheets retreated, the birds probed north, expanding their breeding grounds a little bit each summer, but moving back to warmer climates with the return of each winter. Over time, it is thought, the distance between the ancestral wintering grounds and the breeding rate became greater and greater, until today it reaches from the tropics to the Arctic.

Why go north at all? Why not stay in the balmy southlands, where the climate is kinder, and no arduous migration need be undertaken? There are two reasons: first, competition would inevitably force some ducks north, filling the vacant land and making it their own. But beyond mere emptiness, the high latitudes offer very real advantages – long days (even continuous sunlight in the Arctic) and an abundance of insects, which ducklings need to grow.

The Southern Home theory has the advantage of being neat and logical, but the advocates of the Northern Home theory point out a few holes and inconsistencies in it. For instance, many of the migration corridors followed by waterfowl accurately trace the paths of ancient river systems that predate the glaciers, suggesting a much older heritage for the flyways. Instead, some biologists theorize, the birds originally

lived in the north, which in earlier geologic periods was much warmer than today. The inexplicable change in climate that produced the successive ice ages would have forced the birds south, with northern migration resulting once the glaciers were gone.

In all probability, the truth is somewhere between the two, and in fact many biologists have come to see the Northern Home and Southern Home theories as parts of the same whole, since they are not mutually exclusive. Migration obviously has a lineage that stretches far back in time, but ducks are also capable of remarkable adaptability to changing conditions. Mallards are expanding their breeding range north, for example, while Redheads and Gadwalls are on the march to the east. For the best chance of survival, an innate respect for the past and an ability to meet the future are an invaluable blend.

Even more puzzling than how the flyways started is the question of how ducks find their way from north to south and back again with such uncanny accuracy, especially the young that have never made the journey before. Most of the research conducted so far has involved pigeons, with their proven homing abilities, but it is likely that many of the conclusions apply to all birds to some degree.

Migration takes two different skills, orientation and navigation. The first provides an internal "map" of the land to be crossed; the second is the "compass" by which the bird identifies where it is and the heading it should take to reach its destination.

The basic internal map is apparently instinctive, although adults get lost with less frequency than immatures, suggesting that experience plays a role. In fact, a duck may develop two maps – one genetic, plotting the route of long-distance migration; the other built on experience, useful for finding its way around the immediate territory. The former would lead it 2,000 miles to the tundra, where the latter would then direct it to the same cove on the same tundra pond where it nested the year before.

Studies on pigeons, ducks, songbirds, and seabirds have cleared up some of the confusion about how a bird navigates. All show that birds take their lead from a variety of clues – sometimes relying on one set, sometimes on another. During the day, migrating birds can orient themselves by the sun, instinctively compensating for its changing position from dawn to dark. More important to ducks, which migrate largely at night, is stellar orientation. Research has shown that young birds learn the star patterns of their hatching area, especially the position of the North Star, where apparent rotation is the least. Migrants in the throes of *zugunruhe*, caged in a planetarium, orient themselves properly when shown the stellar pattern with which they grew up. By changing the star map, researchers can change the birds' orientation as well.

A cloudy night makes correct orientation difficult, as does a bright moon (Mallards were shown to orient poorly when the moon was waxing). By day, landmarks, especially major features like river valleys, may coincide with the bird's internal map and lead the way. Pigeons, and possibly other birds as well, can also use the Earth's magnetic field, although magnetic orientation may be of more use close to home than over the long haul. Pigeons and some seabirds also use odor to pinpoint home, but again, such clues may be unavailable or useless to long-distance fliers like ducks. Obviously, there is much still to learn about how ducks find their way.

Migration is a hazardous undertaking, especially for the young of the year, which lack the experience and often the prime physical condition of their parents; among ducks, as with most birds, juvenile mortality in the first fall and winter can reach 75 percent. The causes of death are legion: starvation, disease, injury, predation, and sometimes just plain bad luck. Fog may leave ducks bumbling about blindly, with disastrous consequences should they collide with buildings, utility lines, or transmission towers. A duck flock that is overtaken by a storm may be buffeted by high winds, pummeled mercilessly by hail, or beset by freezing rain that ices its wings and sends it plunging to earth. Serious birders have learned that torrential rainstorms during the migration will ground many migrating ducks, often in unexpected places. Sea ducks like scoters and the Oldsquaw are routinely found waiting out storms on small inland lakes, far from what is considered their normal habitat; the instant the rain abates the ducks are aloft again, so that a bird-watcher who waits for the storm to pass will have missed out on the rarities.

Predators are a danger at all times, although ducks are wary birds by nature, and an open marsh is a difficult place to make a successful stalk. A healthy duck has little to fear from a predator, although the peregrine falcon – the "duck hawk" of the frontier days – is capable of outflying even the fastest waterfowl. Built like a bullet with wings, the falcon can exceed speeds of 200 miles per hour in the lightning-bolt dive known as a stoop, and it routinely preys upon shorebirds, ducks, and other coastal migrants. Faced with such an adversary, the duck's best hope is safety in numbers. A stooping peregrine, confronting a tightly bunched, twisting flock of ducks, will try to cut one from the pack. If it cannot break up the group, its attack will probably fail. Usually, though, the duck that lags behind, or reacts to the alarm an instant too late, is either sick, injured, or stupid, and its removal by a predator from the flock, therefore, is an unwitting service to the population as a whole.

As great a threat as natural predators are the human ones; sport hunters kill hundreds of thousands of ducks during the fall migration each year, within a strict framework of federal and state laws designed to siphon off the biological excess while protecting the species. Hunting has had a fundamental impact on duck conservation and will be discussed in greater detail later.

In autumn, the migrating ducks fly "south," but just how far south is south is relative; some species' wintering grounds are farther north than other species' summer breeding ranges. Many of the sea ducks move no farther south than they must to avoid pack ice, and some eiders scarcely leave the Arctic. Greater Scaups are common in winter as far north as the coast of Newfoundland.

For most of the puddle ducks, there is a more clearly defined break between summer and winter ranges, however. In North America, the Atlantic and Gulf coasts, Mississippi River valley, and Pacific coast are major concentration points. Unlike migrant songbirds, which usually pass the winter in a fairly restricted region, waterfowl tend to have expansive winter ranges; the Blue-winged Teal is found from central

California and the southern Atlantic coast as far south as Peru and Brazil, with the majority wintering in Central America. American Wigeons spread over an even greater area, from southeastern Alaska and Nova Scotia, down both coasts, and from the Gulf through Mexico, the Pacific rim of Central America, and into northern South America.

In the Western Hemisphere, migratory routes usually link North and South America, funneling through the narrow Central America isthmus. Not so in Europe and Asia, where the vastly larger landmass has many more points of passage between north and south – all exploited to some degree by waterfowl. To avoid the dangers of a long water-crossing, most western European migrants follow the bridges (or partial bridges) provided by the Iberian peninsula, Italy, Greece, and the Middle East. There is also considerably more east-west migration than in North America. An example of a duck that migrates in this pattern is the Smew, a type of merganser and one of the world's most striking ducks. Pure white except for black patches on the face, back, and wings, the Smew breeds along freshwater lakes in the northern Soviet Union and Scandinavia. When the bitter arctic winter sets in, Smews migrate to the west and south, seeking out reservoirs, estuaries, and sea coves from Britain to the Black Sea.

The Old World, though, has its share of long-distance migrants. The Garganey, a handsomely marked teal that breeds across Eurasia from Iceland to the Soviet Far East, moves down through the southern European bottleneck in fall to winter in north-central Africa. In keeping with the rule that species that migrate the longest distances tend to stray off course most often, Garganeys are fairly regular vagrants in Alaska and have been recorded on both coasts and a number of inland points in North America.

The Aleutians, all but linking the Old World and the New, boast more than their share of out-of-range birds, including waterfowl. In addition to the Garganey, birders visiting the island chain in fall look for the Falcated Teal, an Asian species named for the drake's long, curving (falcated) tertial feathers, and the Baikal Teal, one of the most distinctively patterned waterfowl in the world; the drake's white, buff, black, and green head appears almost clownlike.

Puddle ducks tend to choose the same habitat in winter that they frequent in summer, although brackish or salt marshes often replace their freshwater counterparts. Not so the diving and sea ducks, which make a radical change from one season to the next. The Surf Scoter –"skunkhead" to New England fishermen – forsakes the ponds of the boreal forest for the waters of both coasts, joining Black and White-winged Scoters, Goldeneyes, Oldsquaws, and Buffleheads. The Surf Scoter favors the surf line, forming huge flocks called rafts just beyond the breakers and diving with impunity through the frigid waves to beds of blue mussels, its primary winter food (one dead Scoter was found to have more than 1,000 small mussels in its stomach). With its odd black, white, and orange bill, the Surf Scoter has attracted a raft of nicknames, as well, among them goggle-nose, sea coot, spectacled coot, butter-billed coot, patch-polled duck, and snuff-taker.

The winter ocean along the northern coast would not seem to be a kindly place to spend several months, but that doesn't stop many species of ducks. For the Common Eider, the changing seasons bring little, if any, migration, and many simply hunker down on the storm-lashed rocks of coastal Alaska or the Canadian Maritime Provinces and wait the winter out. The world's four species of eiders are the most persistently northern ducks; only the Common Eider has significant breeding territory below the Arctic Circle, as far south as Maine and France. They are all superbly adapted to harsh conditions, insulated beneath thick coats of down, and built like most arctic animals, with a relatively massive body and short appendages to conserve heat.

The eiders are bizarrely beautiful. The King Eider drake has a powder-blue head with a greenish cheek patch, a reddish bill, and a bulbous orange beak shield; the Spectacled Eider drake's head is pale green, with a large white eye patch edged in black. Pastel colors are the rule among eiders, with buff and faint greens very common. Living as they do in the world of polar bears and beluga whales, the eiders are little-known to most people – even to most biologists, who have yet to unlock many of the mysteries of their lives. All are pelagic in the winter, particularly the Spectacled Eider, which is presumed to spend the season drifting the Bering Sea, far from shore, diving for mollusks. The King Eider, which winters off Alaska and eastern Canada, is also a shellfish eater, diving to nearly 200 feet for food, a depth exceeded only by the Oldsquaw.

To the strangely patterned Harlequin Duck, the only constant between summer and winter is violent water. During the breeding season, Harlequins inhabit the roughest rivers of the East Canadian Arctic, and from the Rocky Mountains to Alaska, raw-boned, turbulent rivers and streams where the current pounds against the banks, churning itself to foam. The Harlequins brave the maelstrom without a second thought, however, diving to the bottom, where they walk carefully among the rocks, feeding on crustaceans and insects.

In winter, Harlequins flee the remote rivers for the northern Atlantic and Pacific coasts, taking up stations in the roughest surf, wherever the waves hammer the rocky shore or grind against stone jetties. Unlike many diving ducks, which use only their feet to propel them through the water, the Harlequin swims using both legs and wings – perhaps a behavioral adaptation forced on the duck by the exceptionally vicious currents it must fight.

Finally, there are the ducks that stay put, the resident species that have given up the twice-yearly grind of migration in favor of a permanent home. Individuals of many species may take this course (Mallards are notorious stay-at-homes, and Wood Ducks are resident in much of the South), but only a few species have made it a rule rather than an exception.

As might be expected, the resident species are southern in distribution, at least in North America. The whistling ducks, those gangly crossovers between ducks and swans, are non-migratory over most of their range, although the Black-bellied Whistling Duck migrates from Mexico into southern Arizona each summer. The Fulvous Whistling Duck, found in Florida, the Gulf Coast, and southern California, pretty much stays put. Whistling ducks are different from typical ducks in almost every aspect of their anatomy and biology. For example, they feed mostly by night and have partially reversed sexual roles, whereby the male usually incubates the eggs.

Another Gulf Coast resident, the Mottled Duck, may be no more than a subspecies of the Mallard, an argument for taxonomists to bicker over. From an ecological perspective, the Mottled Duck is quite distinct, having given up migration in favor of year-round living in brackish and freshwater marshes. Resembling a Black Duck more than a Mallard, both the male and female Mottled Duck appear identical, with a brown body, pale head, and yellow bill. Until recently, a darker form known as the Mexican Duck was recognized by ornithologists, but it has since been reassigned as a subspecies of the Mallard.

Conservation

It is a statement as seemingly contradictory as it is true: Ducks have thrived precisely because so many people enjoy hunting them. If they didn't decoy well, taste good, and offer an exciting day's sport, North America's waterfowl might have gone the way of the passenger pigeon a long time ago.

But humans cherish those things of immediate value, and ducks have tremendous value to millions of people – to men and women who are willing to endure hours of bone-aching cold in a marsh, the exertion of setting decoys on a heaving salt cove, or a morning-long wait in muddy, damp discomfort, hunched behind a blown-down tree trunk waiting for the flight to come by. These people are also willing to pay millions of dollars for conservation in the form of wetlands acquisition, the creation of refuges, pollution control, and other protective measures.

Call it altruism or enlightened self-interest, but by whatever name, it works. In the face of drought, rampant habitat loss, environmental degradation, and a host of other evils, ducks have sailed through to the tail end of the twentieth century with remarkably few problems, largely because of a multitude of human supporters, who collect their fee each fall in a ritual as old as humanity.

The picture is not nearly as rosy as it once was, but a century ago the situation was considerably worse. Ducks were anybody's game, anytime. There were virtually no laws regulating the length of the hunting season, the bag limit, or the methods of hunting. Market gunners, aiming into sleeping flocks with boat-mounted cannons called punt guns, would kill and cripple hundreds of birds with a single blast. The use of bait and live decoys was rampant, as was spring hunting. Except for the brief nesting season in the northern marshes and forests, there was no letup, no respite.

Still, ducks are biologically resilient, with each hen capable of producing broods of 15 or more chicks a year, a capacity that at least took the edge off the annual, unchecked carnage. But combined with the shooting was an equal toll wrought unintentionally through habitat destruction. Farmers had turned the North American prairies into the world's richest breadbasket, and they did so at the expense of the natural wetlands that made this region sparkle to the eyes of a flying duck.

Legal protection for the ducks came first. Sport hunters, alarmed at the galloping pace of the unchecked killing and the fast-dwindling stocks of ducks, lobbied hard for limits and closed seasons. Complicating matters, however, was the duck's sublime ignorance of borders; a teal may hop across three national boundaries and a dozen state and provincial lines between its wintering grounds and breeding range. Ducks are an international treasure and therefore require an international approach to their protection.

After long negotiations, the Migratory Bird Treaty of 1916 was signed between Canada and the United States, and it was implemented two years later when Congress passed enforcement legislation; a similar treaty with Mexico followed in 1936. Although the treaties covered all migratory birds, from songbirds to sandpipers, they had a tremendous effect on waterfowl. Destructive practices like market gunning were outlawed, since it was declared illegal to sell wild birds, their meat, or body parts. More importantly, it finally gave the federal government power to set seasons and bag limits, putting control of the continent's wildlife in the hands of professional wildlife managers.

Today, duck management is a finely tuned science, combining space-age technology like satellite surveillance of nesting habitats and radio-tracking of tagged birds with old-fashioned field work. Each summer, biologists in the U.S. and Canada conduct a massive survey of the nesting range, estimating the continental duck population, looking for signs of trouble, and providing the data on which decisions about seasons and bag limits should be based. If a particular species is showing signs of trouble, wildlife managers will tighten its protection, as has been the case, off and on for more than 30 years, with the Canvasback, which has suffered from the destruction of its prairie nesting habitat. By regulating hunting so that the breeding population is not reduced, managers try to keep duck numbers stable or increasing, while allowing hunters their sport – a pastime that pumps tens of millions of dollars each year into habitat protection.

But no amount of regulation could undo the damage that had been done to duck habitats in the early years of the twentieth century. That required money, and with the country sliding headlong through the Great Depression and a massive drought, money was as scarce as a water-filled marsh. A number of ideas for raising funds for ducks were floated, but only one caught on – the concept of a national duck-hunting license. Thus the federal Migratory Bird Hunting and Conservation Stamp was born.

Known universally as "the duck stamp," it debuted in 1934 and cost one dollar. The oversized stamp, carrying a drawing of two Mallards, created by noted conservation cartoonist J. N. "Ding" Darling, was required of all waterfowl hunters over the age of 16 and immediately raised more than half a million dollars. Over the years the price of the stamp has steadily increased (to $12.50 in 1990), and the annual revenue figure has climbed to around $15 million, thanks to purchases by hunters, bird-watchers, and collectors smitten by each year's new painting of North American waterfowl. The duck stamp program has been a godsend for wildlife in general, and ducks in particular. The money is used for habitat acquisition and protection, most of it wetlands now part of the National Wildlife Refuge System.

Unlike national parks, which are set aside to preserve areas of lasting scenic value, America's national wildlife refuges are created to preserve habitats vital to wildlife. While the philosophy of "multiple use" may allow such diverse activities as grazing and timbering on refuges (sometimes in excess), the well-being of a refuge's wildlife is supposed to be its guiding principle. There are nearly 400 refuges scattered across the country, with a heavy majority featuring wetlands – and ducks – as the reason for their existence.

Increasingly, the national wildlife refuges, along with similar state wildlife areas and a smattering of private sanctuaries, are the only quality habitats left for ducks, particularly on the wintering grounds. Coastal development and destruction of river bottomlands through draining and damming have destroyed hundreds of thousands of acres of formerly excellent habitats, squeezing more and more birds into smaller and smaller pockets of untouched wetlands. The crowding means more competition for food resources, stress, and a higher rate of disease.

National wildlife refuges largely protect wintering quarters, since the breeding grounds in Canada are beyond the reach of U.S. government funds. But the same sense of Dust Bowl desperation that spawned the duck stamp concept also brought forth Ducks Unlimited, a private group founded in 1937 by a cadre of enlightened waterfowl hunters determined to restore duck populations. Since its inception, DU has made its reputation by raising money among waterfowl hunters, mostly in the U.S., and spending it to protect and enhance breeding marshes in Canada; in recent years the organization has greatly expanded its scope, funding major habitat projects in the U.S. and Mexico, where many ducks winter. Because it is private, DU can spend its money beyond the borders of the U.S., giving it more freedom to act than the federal government.

By using the same kind of water-control devices that were once used to drain wetlands for farming, Ducks Unlimited restores marshes and potholes, creating ideal breeding habitats for ducks, as well as the host of birds, mammals, reptiles, amphibians, and plants that also depend on wetlands. Nevertheless, refuges, DU projects, and other formal waterfowl havens only produce a fraction of the continent's ducks. Most are reared on private land – land held and managed for purposes other than bird conservation, which has caused serious problems for the duck.

Agriculture has been the biggest stumbling block over the years. In the pothole region, which covers more than 300 thousand square miles from Iowa to Manitoba, and once may have held more than 25 million ponds and marshes, farming has taken a terrible toll on the wetlands. By some estimates, as many as 70 percent of the potholes in the Canadian prairie provinces have been destroyed, and even higher destruction has taken place in the upper Midwest. Even in the Dakotas, where a larger percentage of pothole marshes have survived, almost all have suffered some degree of degradation, usually as a result of mowing, livestock grazing, or burning off vegetation that surrounds the water.

To a hen duck, the pothole's surroundings are as important as the water itself, essential for nesting and brooding cover. As the cover is removed, the birds become literally "sitting ducks" for predators; many eggs never survive to hatching, and the ducklings stand a slim chance of making it to adulthood. Biologists have learned that at least 20 percent of the nests must be successful each year in order to maintain the population, but in the bruised and battered potholes, the number of successful nests barely reaches 10 percent.

With the pothole region's long history of agricultural abuse of wetlands, North America's ducks were ripe for a disaster. It came in the 1980's, in the form of a prolonged drought.

Drought is nothing new on the prairies; one of the reasons ducks produce large clutches is to bounce back quickly from such natural disasters, as they did following a drought in the 1960's. But the drought of the 1980's was different – not because of nature, but because of humankind. With so many marshes and ponds already drained and rendered useless, millions of ducks found themselves with no place to breed. Hens bunched up in the few remaining oases offering water, only to find their predators, too, had bunched up. In many areas, nesting success was almost nonexistent year after year. The bottom dropped out of North America's duck population, which plunged from a fall average of 100 million ducks in the 1950's to fewer than 62 million by the middle of the 1980's.

The crash obviously did not affect all species, or all areas of North America, equally. Except for the puzzling decline of the Black Duck, waterfowl production in the East remained high, as did populations in Alaska and the Yukon, an exceptionally fertile area. But in the heartland, the story was bleak, with Pintails and Blue-winged Teal at all-time lows and numbers of Mallards, Redheads, and other diving ducks way down.

Wildlife managers responded by clamping down on hunting, which for the first time threatened to erode breeding stocks. Seasons and bag limits were severely curtailed, and there were calls by many hunters to close the seasons entirely; waterfowlers were asked by conservation groups to voluntarily stop hunting ducks, or to restrict their shooting to drakes only, leaving the hens to breed. Fortunately, many did just that.

But even when drought conditions eased at the end of the decade, ducks did not show the expected rebound. Too much habitat had been lost, and the breeding population had in some cases dropped too low to permit a rapid recovery. In the view of many experts, it will require a major rethinking of land values, away from a philosophy that disparages wetlands as useless and toward one that recognizes their economic as well as environmental value, before duck populations can again reach their previous levels.

In recent years, most of the attention has focused on the breeding grounds, but there is growing concern about the winter quarters of many ducks. Louisiana, for instance, has some of the densest concentrations of wintering waterfowl in the United States, thanks to the Mississippi basin and delta system, which accounts for nearly a quarter of all the wetlands remaining in the U.S. For centuries, the great river carried sediment down from the center of the continent and deposited it along the delta, slowly building the marshes. Major changes in the management of the Mississippi – flood control devices, erosion control measures on tributaries, and perhaps worst of all, a ship channel that shunts the main flow into the Gulf, bypassing the delta – have robbed the marshes of their replenishing dose of silt.

Combined with a rise in the water level of the Gulf, the Louisiana delta is washing away at a rate of 60 square miles a year. The damage goes far beyond ducks, of course, affecting the hundreds of species of birds, mammals, and plants that make up the natural coastal community. Unless sediment is rerouted back to the delta where it belongs, one of North America's most vital wintering grounds will soon be a memory.

One of the most troubling (and mystifying) duck problems in recent years has been the steady decline of the Black Duck. Once the acknowledged monarch of the Atlantic Flyway, the Black was all but revered by waterfowlers for its speed, agility, and most of all, its intelligence; the most sagacious, wary, and wildest of all ducks is how one writer described the species. A hunter who could consistently call in the old, adult "red-legs" was held in high esteem by peers.

Found only in the Northeast, the Black Duck breeds from the Hudson Bay to Newfoundland and south to the Chesapeake, wintering in much the same area but retreating from the northern extremes of its range and dropping down as far as Arkansas and South Carolina. In winter, Black Ducks are frequently associated with the tidal marshes of the mid-Atlantic coast, where Black Duck hunting once took on an almost religious intensity. For generations, Blacks made up the bulk of the eastern flight. Coming from the unmapped forests of Canada, they enjoyed a breeding range largely beyond humans' damaging influence, and hunting regulations (and the species' innate caution) kept winter mortality well within the limits of what the population could stand.

But by the 1960's, it was becoming obvious that something had gone wrong with the Black Duck. The fall flight sagged year after year, and the decline accelerated in the late 1970's and early 1980's; by 1982, for instance, the Black Duck population in Maine had declined by an alarming 75 percent.

No one has yet pinned the blame firmly on any one cause, although there are a number of suspected reasons. The Black Duck's range coincides almost exactly with the region suffering the worst effects of acid precipitation. While elevated pH levels in ponds and lakes might not directly harm the ducks, the acidified waters suffer a loss of plant growth and insect life, so that Black Ducks that nest on them may see their chicks starve before their eyes.

Nor is the trackless northern forest quite as trackless as it used to be. Timbering has long been a major industry in the North Woods, and development has made significant inroads in New England and southern Canada. Chemical spraying to control spruce budworm has also been implicated in the Black Duck's problems. The ducks also do not tolerate disturbance very well, and many abandon traditional breeding areas if human use becomes too great.

Worse, by opening the woods, humans have paved the way for the Mallard. The world's most adaptable duck, the Mallard is not one to let a new opportunity go by, and it has been expanding its range northeast in recent decades, plowing right into the heart of what was once exclusively the Black Duck's domain. Biologists worry that the aggressive Mallards are literally swamping the retiring Black Ducks; the two are almost genetically identical and hybridize with worrisome ease. As Black Duck numbers decrease and the number of Mallards increases, the remaining Blacks tend to mate with their more common cousins at a greater rate, heightening the problem.

Restrictive hunting regulations that reduced the limit and shortened the season for Black Ducks made an immediate difference, suggesting that overhunting may have also been a contributing cause to their decline, but biologists worry that there is little humans can easily do to protect the Black Duck. Banning the release of pen-reared Mallards in the Black's range, as well as reducing the exploding numbers of snow geese on the Atlantic Flyway (which compete with Blacks for food on the coastal wintering grounds), may help, but it is far from certain that the Black Duck will enjoy the same resurgence as the Wood Duck, one of North America's conservation success stories.

There is little argument that a drake Wood Duck, as showy as a rainbow, is one of the prettiest birds on the continent. His head is metallic green, spilling into a long crest lined with white; his chest is maroon; his sides a delicate shade of lemon yellow; and his back iridescent blue and bronze. Even his eye is colorful, a shimmering fleck of blood red.

Woodies, as they are almost universally known, were originally among the most common ducks of the Atlantic Flyway. Aptly named, Wood Ducks inhabit forested streams, rivers, and lakes, shunning open marshes in favor of beaver ponds or flooded woodlands, where they dabble for acorns, seeds, and aquatic insects. They are cavity nesters, completely dependent upon woodpecker holes, squirrel dens, or other natural nest sites – the sort of cavities that usually occur in mature trees.

When the logging industry swept across the Northeast in the nineteenth century, the old den trees growing in accessible stream valleys were among the first to be cut. Even worse, the Wood Duck lacks the guile of the Black Duck and the Mallard, and decoys easily. Good to eat and coveted for its feathers (which were used, as they are today, to make elegant trout flies), the Woodie was ruthlessly pursued. By the beginning of the twentieth century, it was on the verge of extinction, so the Migratory Bird Treaty came just in time. Wood Ducks enjoyed total protection until 1941, when a limited open season on them was reinstated.

The road back was not without trouble. In 1938, a major hurricane blew through the Northeast, toppling many of the remaining nest trees, once again leaving the Woodie in dire straits. But by this time, wildlife managers had realized that Wood Ducks took readily to artificial nest boxes placed in suitable habitats. The new homes were a hit and, over the years, millions have been built and erected by state and federal wildlife agencies, sports clubs, birding organizations, and private landowners, with astonishing results. Much less territorial than many ducks, Woodies will even nest in "apartment" boxes that double or quadruple the potential nesting population – and because nest boxes can be placed on predator-proof poles, nesting success is often substantially higher than in natural cavities. As a result, the Wood Duck is once again common in the East, delighting birders and hunters alike.

A similar program might conceivably help the Mandarin Duck, an Asian species that is, possibly, even more beautiful than the Wood Duck. The Mandarin and the Woodie are obviously close relatives; the females are identical, and freely mate with drakes of either species; drake Mandarins, however, are extravagantly plumaged, with flowing, chestnut facial plumes and orange tertial feathers that flare up above the wings like fans.

Like Wood Ducks, Mandarins nest in hollow trees from China through the Soviet Far East. However, modern forestry practices and emphasis on logging old-growth timber has greatly reduced the number of suitable nest trees, and the Mandarin Duck is declining dramatically in the wild. Luckily, it has been a favorite of exotic bird lovers and zoo keepers for more than a century and is widespread in parks and private collections; it has also been introduced to the wild in Great Britain, where it is now rather common.

Human activity obviously can have a profoundly devastating impact on wildlife, ducks included, but the sword cuts both ways, and for some species the results can be positive. In Great Britain, the construction of hydroelectric dams created large bodies of water in regions that had previously lacked natural lakes. These, in turn, attracted Tufted Ducks, close relatives of the Scaup.

Unknown as a breeding bird in Britain prior to 1849, the Tufted Duck is now the island's most common diving duck, nesting along reservoirs, abandoned gravel pits, and municipal park lakes. The Tufted Duck got a further assist by the accidental introduction to Britain of the zebra mussel, an Asian mollusk that has taken over many lakes, providing the ducks with food. Interestingly, the zebra mussel is now established in the Great Lakes; biologists fear it may force out native species, but its potential impact on waterfowl is unknown.

Wildlife conservation can seem like an endless series of battles, and duck conservation is no different. But if the last years of the twentieth century have not been the best for ducks, they at least hold the promise of better times ahead. With the rise in environmental awareness, people have begun to realize the value inherent in wetlands and all the creatures that depend on them. No longer are birders and hunters the only voices calling for the protection of swamps, marshes, and bogs – engineers have come to recognize them for their flood control abilities and farmers for the way they store water against drought. Municipalities, which once would have used local marshes as convenient landfills, now look to them as effective filters for treated city sewage, and a number of towns have gone so far as to build artificial marshes near their treatment plants, actually creating a duck habitat in the process.

In the end, it is a matter of will. The problems facing ducks are not insurmountable, but they do require unified action on the part of sportspeople, birders, farmers, and the general public. Neither are the solutions without expense, but, then, who can put a price tag on the sight of a male Wood Duck preening in a shaft of afternoon light, or on a flock of Canvasbacks rending the dawn air? Wild ducks, with their grace, beauty, and the freedom of spirit they provide us, are priceless – and we should not skimp on their preservation.

Preceding pages: With a kick and a splash, a drake Northern Pintail leaps into the air. He is easily recognized by his brown head and slender, white neck. *This page, above:* Although her colors are not as bold as her mate's, this Northern Pintail female, followed closely by her brood of newly hatched ducklings, has the same slender neck. *Opposite:* Three Northern Pintails circle over the rugged landscape of Alaska as they return from their wintering grounds, perhaps as far away as Mexico. With stops along the way, such a journey may take as long as three months.

One of the most graceful of all the dabbling ducks, the Northern Pintail is probably one of the most numerous. There may be as many as 6 million in North America, and millions more in Europe and Asia.

With only a hint of the intricate pattern of colors he'll soon be wearing, this Northern Pintail is nearing the end of a midsummer molt. During this time his feathers will fall out and be completely replaced by new ones. The brief loss of his wing feathers will cause the Pintail to become flightless for several weeks.

Preceding page: Newly paired Northern Pintails at their wintering grounds. The mated drake has his head slightly raised, a subtle signal that he is fully prepared to do battle with any rival that tries to supplant him. *This page:* The long, broad bill of the Northern Shoveler, *Anas clypeata,* sets it apart from other North American ducks. The fresh feathers of this female indicate that she has completed her summer molt and is ready to begin the long migration south. *Below:* This Northern Shoveler has only just begun molting and displays many worn feathers. During the molt, its drab plumage will be replaced by brightly colored feathers.

Drawing water in at the front of its bill, a Northern Shoveler filters out seeds, small snails, and aquatic insects. Strained water flows out from the sides of its bill. All dabbling ducks feed in this way, but the Shoveler's bill is the most highly adapted for this method. *Below:* Despite their distinctive bills, Northern Shovelers are closely related to Blue-winged Teal, *Anas discors*, as the pale-blue patch on the outstretched wings of this female Shoveler reveals.

This drake Northern Shoveler has nearly completed its summer molt. The green head and chestnut flanks of its nuptial plumage are fully visible, but it is still wearing a few of the brown-barred feathers of its eclipse plumage.

Preceding page: A new arrival to the breeding grounds in southeastern Alaska, this Northern Shoveler, its yellow eye seemingly glowing, rests in shallow water among a host of horsetails. *Above:* With wings outstretched and neck held forward, a Northern Shoveler alights on the water.

Cinnamon Teal, *Anas cyanoptera,* inhabit shallow marshes in mountain areas and open country, feeding on seeds, stems, insects, and mollusks. *Left:* Unlike most dabbling ducks which form pairs in the fall, Cinnamon Teal do not begin mating until spring. The drake does not acquire his bright colors until late winter, months after other dabbling duck drakes do. *Opposite:* As the sun rises over a lake bordered by marsh grass, hardly a ripple disturbs the surface of the water. Soon winter will arrive and the ducks that have found food here will head south to a warmer climate.

Although his red eye remains wide open, this Cinnamon Teal has buried his bill among the feathers of his back, a sign that he may soon fall asleep. The slightest sound will wake him, and judging from his alert expression, such a sound may have just interrupted a nap.

Green-winged Teal, *Anas crecca*, are the smallest of the dabbling ducks and probably the fastest. *Below:* Green-winged Teal fly swiftly between a variety of feeding habitats, from freshwater marshes to upland woods, where they have been found walking among the trees collecting acorns.

The nest of a Blue-winged Teal is typical of the dabbling ducks; it is a cradle of soft down pulled from the female's breast, and a clutch of up to 15 cream-colored eggs. *Opposite:* Many ducks and other waterfowl are noted for their wedge or arc-shaped flight formations, but on short flights, they often fly in what appears to be a disorganized bunch.

Preceding pages: With a kick and a splash, a drake Northern Pintail leaps into the air. He is easily recognized by his brown head and slender, white neck. *This page, above:* Although her colors are not as bold as her mate's, this Northern Pintail female, followed closely by her brood of newly hatched ducklings, has the same slender neck. *Opposite:* Three Northern Pintails circle over the rugged landscape of Alaska as they return from their wintering grounds, perhaps as far away as Mexico. With stops along the way, such a journey may take as long as three months.

Preceding page: Newly paired Northern Pintails at their wintering grounds. The mated drake has his head slightly raised, a subtle signal that he is fully prepared to do battle with any rival that tries to supplant him. *This page:* The long, broad bill of the Northern Shoveler, *Anas clypeata,* sets it apart from other North American ducks. The fresh feathers of this female indicate that she has completed her summer molt and is ready to begin the long migration south. *Below:* This Northern Shoveler has only just begun molting and displays many worn feathers. During the molt, its drab plumage will be replaced by brightly colored feathers.

Drawing water in at the front of its bill, a Northern Shoveler filters out seeds, small snails, and aquatic insects. Strained water flows out from the sides of its bill. All dabbling ducks feed in this way, but the Shoveler's bill is the most highly adapted for this method. *Below:* Despite their distinctive bills, Northern Shovelers are closely related to Blue-winged Teal, *Anas discors*, as the pale-blue patch on the outstretched wings of this female Shoveler reveals.

This drake Northern Shoveler has nearly completed its summer molt. The green head and chestnut flanks of its nuptial plumage are fully visible, but it is still wearing a few of the brown-barred feathers of its eclipse plumage.

Preceding page: **A new arrival to the breeding grounds in southeastern Alaska, this Northern Shoveler, its yellow eye seemingly glowing, rests in shallow water among a host of horsetails.** *Above:* **With wings outstretched and neck held forward, a Northern Shoveler alights on the water.**

Cinnamon Teal, *Anas cyanoptera,* inhabit shallow marshes in mountain areas and open country, feeding on seeds, stems, insects, and mollusks. *Left:* Unlike most dabbling ducks which form pairs in the fall, Cinnamon Teal do not begin mating until spring. The drake does not acquire his bright colors until late winter, months after other dabbling duck drakes do. *Opposite:* As the sun rises over a lake bordered by marsh grass, hardly a ripple disturbs the surface of the water. Soon winter will arrive and the ducks that have found food here will head south to a warmer climate.

Although his red eye remains wide open, this Cinnamon Teal has buried his bill among the feathers of his back, a sign that he may soon fall asleep. The slightest sound will wake him, and judging from his alert expression, such a sound may have just interrupted a nap.

Green-winged Teal, *Anas crecca,* are the smallest of the dabbling ducks and probably the fastest. *Below:* Green-winged Teal fly swiftly between a variety of feeding habitats, from freshwater marshes to upland woods, where they have been found walking among the trees collecting acorns.

The nest of a Blue-winged Teal is typical of the dabbling ducks; it is a cradle of soft down pulled from the female's breast, and a clutch of up to 15 cream-colored eggs. *Opposite:* Many ducks and other waterfowl are noted for their wedge or arc-shaped flight formations, but on short flights, they often fly in what appears to be a disorganized bunch.

Blue-winged Teal like reedy ponds and can often be found resting on half-submerged logs. Like the Cinnamon Teal, they don't begin to form pairs until late winter, but the pair bond is strong, and incubation is usually well along before the drake finally leaves his mate.

With a smooth, gray head and a bold, white crescent in front of each eye, the drake Blue-winged Teal is one of the most elegant ducks. They look very different from Cinnamon Teal drakes, but females of the two species are almost impossible to tell apart.

The Baikal Teal, *Anas formosa*, named for Lake Baikal in Siberia, is an Asian species that occasionally wanders to Alaska and the West Coast, as well as to northern Europe. Its closest relative among North American ducks is the Green-winged Teal. *Opposite:* A common plant in shallow ponds throughout eastern North America, pickerelweed has blue-violet flowers in summer and early fall. The flowers give way to small fruits, each one containing a single seed; these are a favorite food of many ducks.

The Baikal Teal has been known to reach the Pacific coast of North America on its own, but birds that have turned up in the eastern states of New Jersey, North Carolina, Ohio, and Pennsylvania are thought to have escaped from captivity.

Although the Gadwall, *Anas strepera,* is seldom seen in large numbers, there are probably well over a million in North America and throughout Eurasia. Both populations remain almost exclusively on freshwater, and prefer quiet ponds and marshes for nesting and rearing young. *Below:* Like other ducks, female Gadwalls accompany their young from the time they hatch until they are old enough to fly. Young Gadwalls must sometimes be escorted long distances overland because the females may build their nests far from water.

Preceding pages: With most dabbling ducks, the drake abandons his mate and begins molting while the female is incubating her eggs. Among Gadwalls, however, pairs will sometimes stay together even after the male has begun to molt. *Insert:* Gadwalls like shallow water with lots of vegetation and they often hide among the plants. *This page, above:* While a drake Gadwall is not as dramatically patterned as other ducks, he is a quietly elegant bird, with soft gray flanks, a sandy-colored head, and black around the tail. *Opposite:* Another name for the American Wigeon, *Anas americana,* is "baldpate," given to it because of the white patch on the top of the heads of drakes. It is an unusual dabbling duck, obtaining much of its plant food by stealing it from diving ducks and other duck-like birds.

The female American Wigeon lacks the bold head pattern of the male, but shares the blue-gray bill tipped with black, which makes her easy to identify. Her flanks are usually rusty and brighter than in the drake.

The European Wigeon, *Anas penelope,* is an occasional visitor to most parts of North America. Like its American cousin, it feeds by dabbling, but also robs other birds of plants they have brought to the surface after a dive.

The American Black Duck, *Anas rubripes*, resembles the Mallard, although it is a bit darker, and the legs of adult drakes are red or orange. *Below:* Black Ducks are found only in North America, where they gather food by dabbling, wading, and grazing on land.

Male and female Black Ducks are nearly identical; they can be distinguished by their different bill colors: olive-gray in the female and yellow in the male. *Overleaf:* **When the marsh grass turns gold in the fall, it is a signal that many seeds have fallen into the shallow water, and that the marsh is now a good feeding place for ducks of many species.**

Bay Ducks

Preceding pages: The Common Merganser, *Mergus merganser,* has a long slender bill, which serves a different purpose than the broad and flat bill of most ducks. Common Mergansers are diving ducks that seize fish and they hold their slippery prey with sharp "teeth" along the edge of their bills. *This page, left:* Nestled among the feathers of its mother, a newly-hatched Common Merganser has an intricate pattern of stripes on its face, and already has the long, serrated bill it will need to catch fish when it reaches maturity. *Below:* Unlike the female, which has a rusty head and ragged crest, the drake Common Merganser has a green head with a crest that is barely visible. The long, red bill and flashing, white breast and flanks make this dweller of lakes and large rivers easy to distinguish from the Mallard, which also has a green head. *Opposite:* Taking a rest from pursuing fish in the swift current of a river, a female Common Merganser reveals the slender body and powerful feet that give it speed and agility during its underwater hunts.

Preceding pages: A female Red-breasted Merganser, *Mergus serrator*, her bill more slender and her head a duller shade of rust than the female Common Merganser, stands and flaps her wings. Red-breasted Mergansers winter almost exclusively on saltwater, occasionally even straying out of sight of land. *Insert:* The breast of the drake Red-breasted Merganser is not actually red; it is pale rusty-brown and streaked with black. During the summer, these saltwater fishing ducks nest on lakes and rivers near the edge of the Arctic tundra. *Above:* Hooded Mergansers, *Mergus cucullatus*, are birds of forested lakes and rivers. Smaller than the other Mergansers, they prey chiefly on minnows, and also include aquatic insects in their diet.

The crest of this female Hooded Merganser will rise and fall according to her mood. With hood lifted and fanned, something has apparently alarmed or annoyed her. Staring straight at the camera, she has spotted the lens and is prepared to dart away. *Below:* Although not entirely confident that there is no danger, the bird has tucked her bill into the feathers of her back and appears ready to close her watchful eyes.

This young Hooded Merganser has just popped back to the surface after a dive and is holding a small fish captured during its underwater foray. *Opposite:* Hooded Mergansers spend most of the winter in flocks that are often segregated by sex. These two drakes are at peace, as indicated by their lowered crests. This will change in late winter when pairs form; then the crests will be raised threateningly whenever one male approaches another.

In full nuptial plumage, the drake Hooded Merganser is one of the handsomest ducks. In any plumage, the adult drake can be recognized by his golden-yellow eyes. Since they prefer smaller fish, "hoodies" are often found in shallower water than other Mergansers. *Opposite:* Its crest fully fanned in a display of threat, a drake Hooded Merganser rises and flaps his wings. Although a raised crest can indicate a variety of emotions, drakes seldom raise the crest in the presence of their mates.

Stocky diving ducks, Greater Scaup, *Aytha marila*, have a flightless period of molt in midsummer, just as dabbling ducks do. This female, nearing the end of her molt in Alaska, has not yet acquired all of her long wing-feathers.

The drake Greater Scaup has a glossy, dark-green head and a nearly white back. Before they head for the wintering grounds these birds are often found alone, but once they arrive in the coastal waters of the northern states and Europe, they gather in "rafts" that may number in the thousands.

Both the exclusively American Lesser Scaup, *Aytha affinis*, and the Greater Scaup, shown here, have dark eyes until they are adults, when the eyes become yellow. This young female has begun to acquire the white patch around the bill that is also a sign of adulthood. *Below:* This female Greater Scaup is swimming peacefully on the surface, but drops of water clinging to her feathers show that she has just returned from a dive in search of seeds, crustaceans, or small snails.

Keeping a sharp lookout with its yellow eyes, a Lesser Scaup rests on the water with its bill tucked among the feathers of its back. Lesser Scaup are more abundant in winter in the southern states than the Greater Scaup, and are more numerous overall. *Below:* Drake Lesser Scaup have a head glossed with purple, rather than green like the drake Greater Scaup, and the highest point on the crown is at the back of the head. Aside from these differences, the two are not easy to distinguish.

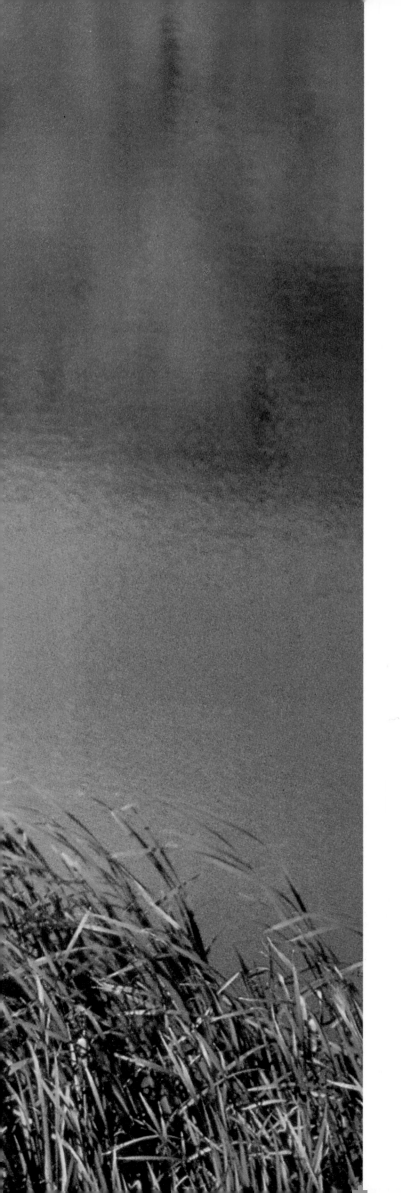

Fall has come to a marshy pond in New Hampshire. Some of the leaves of the cattails in the foreground have turned brown and the reflection of the distant shore in the calm water reveals the autumn colors of maples. *Above:* A pair of Common Goldeneyes swims quietly across a lake. Soon the female will select a suitable cavity in a tree, line it with down, and lay as many as 15 pale-green eggs. *Overleaf:* When young Goldeneyes hatch, they must drop from the nest tree into the water, and follow their mother in pursuit of food. Sometimes the family rests on a log before resuming its travels around the lake.

A Common Goldeneye lifts itself from the surface of the water to flap its wings. When these birds fly their wings make a whistling noise so loud it can be heard in dense fog as a flock passes by far offshore. *Opposite:* The white spot at the base of the bill of the Common Goldeneye can be identified at great distances. These birds are usually seen in winter in flocks, diving repeatedly in search of small crabs, snails, and mussels.

A big stand of healthy cattails is a welcome sight to anyone who loves the outdoors; it is a sign of a healthy marsh, full of aquatic animals and the birds that prey on them.

The Barrow's Goldeneye, *Bucephala islandica*, is much less common than the Common Goldeneye, and nests only in the Rocky Mountains, along the coast of Labrador, and in Iceland. There are fewer than 200 thousand of these birds in North America, while the Common Goldeneye numbers more than a million. *Below:* The drake Barrow's Goldeneye has a white crescent, not a round spot, in front of its eye, and has more black on its back than a Common Goldeneye. It is seldom seen in large flocks like its relative.

Preceding pages: The Canvasback is a large relative of the Scaup. It nests on prairie marshes and winters on open bays and lakes with plentiful vegetation. Amazingly, the birds return year after year to the same feeding grounds. *This page, above:* Canvasbacks are largely vegetarian. Pondweeds, wild celery, and seeds are the main foods of these ducks, but they also eat insects and an occasional fish. *Below:* Female Canvasbacks lack the chestnut, white, and black characteristic of drakes, but their bills have the same sloping profile. Canvasbacks form pairs in late winter or spring, but winter flocks contain both females and drakes.

A drake Canvasback lifts himself up on the water and flaps his powerful wings. Like other diving ducks, Canvasbacks must taxi across the water before they can fly, but once airborne they are one of the fastest species of North American ducks.

Like Canvasbacks, Redheads, *Aytha americana*, raise their broods chiefly on marshes and potholes in the prairies of the Midwest, although some nest as far north as Alaska. *Opposite:* By the time Redheads arrive at their nesting grounds in spring, they are already paired. This pair will be inseparable until incubation begins, and some drakes stay with their mates until the eggs hatch and the family begins to swim about in search of food.

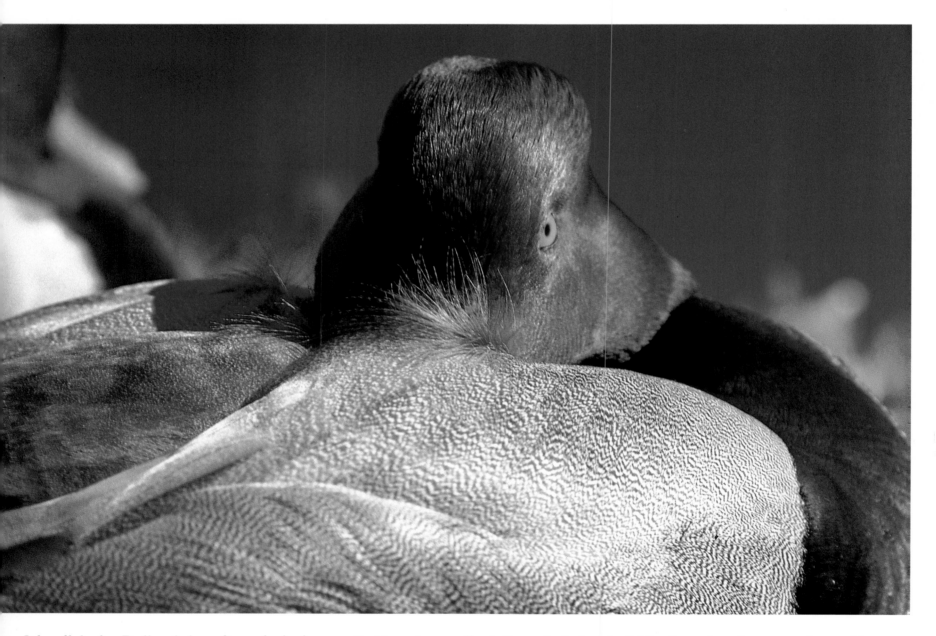

Like all ducks, Redheads have firm, sleek plumage that is water-repellent. Beneath their colorful feathers they also wear a layer of fine, soft down that provides insulation when the birds dive in cold water. *Opposite:* After a long molting period, adult drake Redheads finally acquire their rich, chestnut-red head in late October or November. Young birds take even longer, and do not acquire their nuptial plumage and the bright, blue bill until late in January.

Sea Ducks

Preceding pages: Beyond this broad mudflat on the coast of Oregon the surf is breaking, and in the water beyond, flocks of sea ducks feed. *This page:* On the shores of eastern Canada and northern New England, Common Eiders, *Somateri mollissima,* build their nests in the shelter of the forest. When the ducklings hatch, they join other broods that swim about under the supervision of several females. *Opposite:* The down that lines the nest of the Common Eider is thick and abundant, and for centuries has been gathered to make snug linings for coats and quilts. Although synthetic linings have been developed, real eiderdown is still collected, because the insulation it provides has not yet been matched. *Following pages, insert:* Common Eiders are very large and look bulky and clumsy in flight, as their black-and-white wings flap slowly over the waves. Eiders do not usually fly long distances; birds in warmer latitudes often winter near their nesting grounds. Most of the world's commercial eiderdown is harvested in Iceland, and fortunately the birds tolerate this invasion of their privacy, seldom deserting their nests after the down has been removed.

The shape and color of the shields on the forehead of drake Common Eiders vary, revealing the location of the bird's origin. The broad, greenish shields shown here are the hallmark of the Eiders that nest in eastern Canada and northern New England. *Opposite:* The pointed, orange shields of this drake indicate that he is from the Far North. Some of these arctic birds migrate as far as the coast of New England, where they mingle with local birds.

Although they can be found in winter as far south as New Jersey, King Eiders, *Somateria spectabilis*, nest only in the high Arctic. Here, a pair, newly arrived from their winter quarters, stands on the shore of a tundra pond. *Below:* With his broad, orange shields and powder-blue crown and nape, a drake King Eider is one of the most beautiful of all ducks. King Eiders often mingle with Common Eiders in winter, but the black backs of King Eiders make them easy to identify.

The Harlequin Duck, *Histrionicus histrionicus,* **can be found in winter along rocky, wave-lashed coasts. During the summer, they live on rushing mountain streams, diving for food in the swift current. This female has paused for a breather just below a stretch of rapids.**

It is easy to see how the Harlequin Duck got its name. The bizarre pattern of spots and stripes worn by the drake suggests the makeup of a clown. But the name fails to give credit to this tough little inhabitant of turbulent waters.

Preceding pages: Harlequin Ducks are not very social, and are only rarely seen in flocks. But along the rugged coasts where these birds spend the winter, small groups often climb out of the crashing surf and rest on the rocks together. *This page:* The Oldsquaw, *Clangula hyemalis,* is a true sea duck, able to dive to depths of 200 feet. But like all ducks, they must come ashore to nest. Here a female eyes the camera from her nest, hidden among some dwarf arctic willows.

The drake Oldsquaw is the only North American duck that wears two strikingly different plumages during the year. In summer, the head and neck are mainly black, with white spots on the head; the bill is pink and black. *Below:* In winter, drake Oldsquaws have an even more beautiful plumage. Now largely white, this drake still sports the long, pointed tail feathers he wore during the summer; the bill is still pink and black.

The White-winged or Velvet Scoter, *Melanitta fusca*, is the most abundant Scoter on the East Coast during the winter. These stocky ducks migrate as far south as the Carolinas, traveling in long lines low over the waves. *Above:* The Black or Common Scoter, *Melanitta nigra*, is well named, for it is the only one of the three Scoter species whose plumage is entirely black. Actually only the male is black, with the exception of a bright, yellow knob on the bill that adds a bit of a color.

The Surf Scoter, *Melanitta perspicillata,* is the most common Scoter on the West Coast, wintering from the Aleutian Islands to as far south as northern Mexico. The white patches on the drake's head have given this bird its hunter's name, "skunkhead." *Opposite:* The strong, somewhat hooked bill of the White-winged Scoter is useful when the bird dives for food. Reaching depths of up to 40 feet, this powerful sea duck tears mussels, barnacles, and even oysters loose from the rocks. *Following pages:* Early on a fall morning, a gentle mist rises from the surface of a marshy pond. Such ponds provide vital stopovers for ducks as they head southward to avoid the rigors of winter.

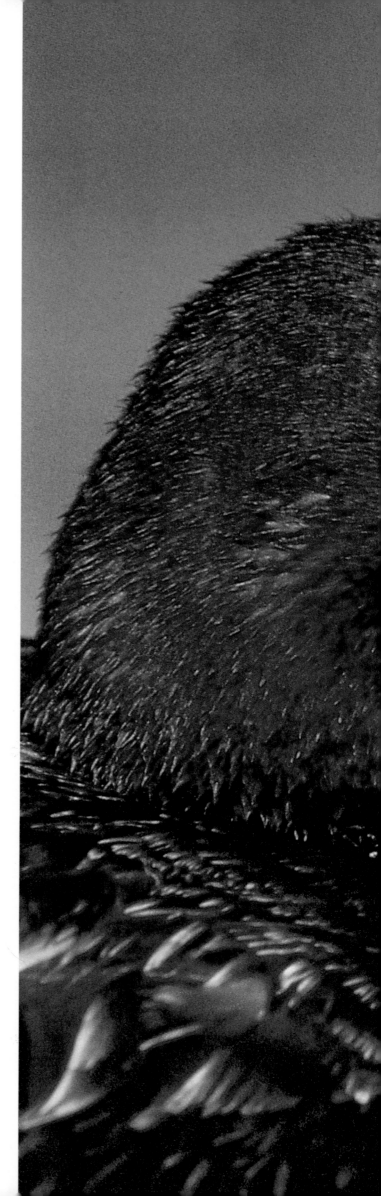

Freshwater Ducks

Preceding page: A drake Wood Duck, *Aix sponsa,* preens while standing on a log beside a woodland pond. Acorns are a major part of the diet of this elegant duck, and if they cannot be found in shallow waters, the Wood Duck will come ashore and seek them on dry land. *Above:* Usually considered the most beautiful duck in North America, the Wood Duck wears rich colors that range from metallic blue, green, and purple to soft buff, and is marked with a trim pattern of white stripes and black bars.

Preceding pages: Pairs of Wood Ducks stay together longer than most other species of ducks. Most birds have mates by October and they don't separate until early in the following summer. Although they are not very social and are usually seen in isolated pairs, Wood Ducks frequently nest close together on ponds where there are numerous tree cavities. *This page:* Female Wood Ducks, lack the bright colors of their mates. They wear a coat of soft grays and browns, and have a broad white ring around their eyes.

When a female Wood Duck flaps her wings, more colors can be seen. The inner wing feathers are glossy-blue like those of the drake, and the feathers under the wing are neatly barred with black and white. *Overleaf:* The Black-bellied Whistling Duck, *Dendrocygna autumnalis,* is a bird of tree-lined ponds and swampy woodlands along the Mexican border, but ranges as far south as Argentina. It often feeds in rice paddies and flooded croplands; the spread of agriculture may have benefited this tropical duck.

With their long legs, long necks, and almost goose-like bills, Black-bellied Whistling Ducks bear little resemblance to most other North American ducks, but the male and female of the species are virtually identical. Whistling ducks are not closely related to other ducks; their nearest allies may be the swans.

The Black-billed Whistling Duck, *Dendrocygna arborea*, a relative of the Black-bellied Whistling Duck, is found only in the West Indies, where it lives in wooded swamps. Although it is protected on all the major islands, the population is declining, and it is probably numerous only in Cuba.

Preceding pages: **Fulvous Whistling Ducks,** *Dendrocygna bicolor,* **which can be found from southern California east to Louisiana and Florida, spend most of their time in the water. But when there is no apparent threat, they will stand and sleep on the shore of a marshy pond during the day.** *This page:* **The Ruddy Duck,** *Oxyura jamaicensis,* **is a chunky diving duck with long, stiff tail-feathers. Perhaps the most aquatic of ducks, it will usually avoid danger by diving rather than taking to the air.**

The drake Ruddy Duck is a handsome bird, with a chestnut body, white cheeks, and bright, blue bill. *Overleaf:* With his tail raised and his head held high, this drake Ruddy Duck is preparing for one of his courtship displays. *Insert:* During the display, the drake Ruddy Duck will bend his tail over his back, dip his bill toward the water, and press air from his breast feathers, causing a cloud of bubbles to appear in front of him.

The Mandarin Duck, *Aix galericulata*, is native to eastern Asia, where fewer than 5,000 pairs survive on rivers and lakes in wooded regions. Fortunately, this elegant duck has been introduced into Britain, where about 2,000 birds now live in the wild.

Opposite: Drake Mandarin Ducks wear a pair of orange "sails," modified wing-feathers over their backs. The Mandarin is closely related to the Wood Duck of North America. While this kinship is not obvious in the elaborate plumage of the drake, it is easy to see in the Mandarin female's resemblance to the female Wood Duck.

REDHEAD

RUDDY DUCK

SCAUP

SCOTER

SHELDUCK

SHOVELER